Joseph's Story

JOSEPH'S TESTIMONY IF GIVEN TODAY
(THE EARTHLY FATHER OF GOD'S SON)

Bonnie Logan

TRILOGY CHRISTIAN PUBLISHERS

TUSTIN, CA

Trilogy Christian Publishers

A Wholly Owned Subsidiary of Trinity Broadcasting Network

2442 Michelle Drive

Tustin, CA 92780

For information, address Trilogy Christian Publishing

Rights Department, 2442 Michelle Drive, Tustin, Ca 92780.

Trilogy Christian Publishing/ TBN and colophon are trademarks of Trinity Broadcasting Network.

For information about special discounts for bulk purchases, please contact Trilogy Christian Publishing.

Manufactured in the United States of America

Trilogy Disclaimer: The views and content expressed in this book are those of the author and may not necessarily reflect the views and doctrine of Trilogy Christian Publishing or the Trinity Broadcasting Network.

10 9 8 7 6 5 4 3 2 1

Library of Congress Cataloging-in-Publication Data is available.

ISBN 978-1-64773-216-5

ISBN 978-1-64773-217-2

Contents

Joseph's Family Painting

The painting of the Holy Family is compliments of artist

Elizabeth Gautsche.

Elizabeth was a great example of a Godly wife, mother, and grandmother.

She never stopped praying for her family and standing on God's Word and covenant promises through her Lord and Savior, Jesus Christ.

Dedication

God the Father, Jesus Christ, and the Holy Spirit

I dedicate this book to my Lord and Savior, Jesus Christ, who has proven His faithfulness and love to me all my life. Even as a prodigal, when I cried out and said, "Dear God, help," He never told me, "You deserve what is happening." He just started to lead me out, and I have never been the same. Thank God for His transforming power. Life experiences have taught me that God's promises never fail, but the best is knowing that I am forgiven and that I have received the promise of eternal life through what Jesus did for us. Everything changed when I accepted His great love for me. I started living in the fact that nothing is impossible with God. His Word never fails, and I can rest in my heavenly Father.

My Parents

The tribute to the artist Elizabeth Gautsche was from my personal experience as her daughter. She stood on the promises of God and believed that God would be faithful to His promises. She never gave up, and I could always count on her love, even when she did not approve of my decisions. During worship one Mother's Day, I opened my eyes to see my sister on one side of my mother and me on the other. All three of us with our arms lifted, worshiping God together. I couldn't help but thank God that He had answered my mother's prayers. My dad was a man of God, and the way he lived his life was proof. When my dad would share his testimony, he would tell how my mom would ask him where they went wrong. My dad would say, "Liz, the Bible says to train up a child in the way he should go, and when he is old, he will not depart from it." I am incredibly thankful that my parents stood on the promises in God's Word, and that God thought I was "old" in my mid-twenties.

My Children

I give thanks every day that the Lord has blessed my life with my three children, Tara, Ryan, and James.

They have taught me and continue to teach me about the blessings and love of God towards us. They are a great encouragement to me, and I can always count on them. We have walked together through good and bad times. We can definitely testify that we have seen the goodness of the Lord in the land of the living.

They have also blessed me with my son-in-law Kent and daughter-in-law Annie, and with four beautiful grandchildren, Tyler, Austin, Brooklyn, and Jaxson.

God has also let me inherit two daughters through marriage and has blessed my life with their families. Even through life changes, God has kept us together.

God showed me years ago that the only blessing He gives you on earth that you can take to heaven with you is your children.

Acknowledgements

I want to give a sincere thank you to the people God has put in my life who have helped to make this book a reality.

Pastor James and his wife Maxine, for being faithful to the Lord. Pastor James carries a great anointing, and they have both been a blessing to my entire family and me.

To my co-worker and friend, Kathy Blessing. Her encouragement and editorial skills were an enormous help in writing this story.

Introduction

I was getting ready for church one Sunday morning, and the Lord spoke to me and said, "I want you to teach the fifth and sixth-grade girls." At that time, I had been teaching the three-to-five-year-olds and a women's home Bible study. I can't explain that Sunday morning, but it was like something leaped in my spirit.

When I started teaching the three-year-old class, I asked the Lord how to teach the children about Christmas. He told me to make cakes and have the children decorate a birthday cake for Jesus. I could write a book about all the experiences from making the cakes and how excited the children were with the birthday cakes they decorated for Jesus.

At Christmas, I asked the Lord, and the Holy Spirit led me to present the story like Mary's testimony to the fifth and sixth-grade girls. We went to Mary's house for tea, and I played the role of Mary. I told them the Christmas story as Mary's life story. It was so well-received and anointed that I couldn't wait to be able to teach that lesson again. Years passed, and I was able to teach it a few more times.

Then I started to teach a Sunday school class in a small church, and I had all the age groups in one class. Only God can anoint a class that all would participate in and enjoy. The class would vary in size each week from five to twenty. After teaching for several years, the week before Christmas I was reading the Christmas story in the Bible, and a thought came to present the story as if I was Joseph, telling from Joseph's perspective what God had done. The next week I would tell the birth of Jesus as Mary telling the story.

Each time I taught, I would ask God to anoint my words and my tongue so all that heard would know Him and be blessed. I would study the Word, but when I played the role of Joseph or Mary, I would ad-lib. The way the Holy Spirit led me the Sunday I did Joseph, and the Word that was taught, were all from the Holy Spirit. I never planned what to say to them, nor did the thought cross my mind before then. I drove home that day from church, amazed at the teaching and the anointing.

The next Sunday, I prepared the cakes so the children could decorate birthday cakes for Jesus. The Bible lesson I prepared was presenting Mary, telling what God had done in her life. Since this was a small church with an attendance of about seventy-five people (including the children), the agenda was different than in the larger churches that I have attended. On this Sunday, the pastor came to me a few minutes before church was to begin and asked if I would be able to teach a special Christmas message to the congregation. I immediately asked God for wisdom and anointing, and I felt the Holy Spirit wanted me to present the message as if I was Joseph, like I had the week before. As I started, the anointing was great, and the powerful message that was given was from the Lord.

The pastor called me the following week and informed me that he had recorded the message on Sunday and had requested that it be played the next Saturday on a local radio broadcast in which some of us were involved. I started to pray, because I knew that a couple of times I had messed up in the wording, and with a few names in the story. I listened on Saturday, and even with the inaccuracies I could feel the anointing, and the message was all about Jesus. The radio program aired every Saturday morning, and the broadcast included a variety of preachers. Well, the radio station made a mistake, and my message aired for three Saturdays in a row.

The pastor gave me a copy of the CD, and every time I played it I would cringe at the mistakes, but I could not deny the anointing and how the Word spoke to me each time I listened. Towards the end of 2015, I felt the Lord telling me to write down the message. With the written message, I was able to correct some of the mistakes I had made when presenting Joseph's testimony live.

Upon starting to put this message into written form, I thought that I was doing the Christmas message for my family. Before we open gifts, I always like to tell or read about the birth of Jesus. Since my parents have gone home to be with the Lord, Christmas is now just my three children and their families. I have found that it is not always easy to tell the Christmas story, and not all the family members are happy to have it shared. As it came closer to Christmas, I still had not written the entire story down. I started to pray and tell the Lord that if I was supposed to give the Christmas story this year, He would need to make a way. A few days before Christmas, my daughter stopped by to discuss the plans for our family Christmas, which was going to be at my youngest son's house on Christmas Eve. We were making sure of the time, food, and gift-giving. Then we started to talk about the agenda, and my daughter said to me, "I have been thinking, Mom, you know how you like to tell the Christmas story? Well, instead of doing it right before we open our gifts, why don't you do it while we are eating? I think the kids would listen better." Our God is a way-maker!

I pray as you read Joseph's testimony that you feel the anointing of the Holy Spirit, and that it ignites a fire in you to worship our Lord and Savior, Jesus Christ, and to look forward to the return of our soon-coming King.

Love,
Bonnie

CHAPTER 1

Jesus Christ's Birth, as Told by Luke and Matthew

Luke 2:1-39 (KJV)

1 And it came to pass in those days, that there went out a decree from Caesar Augustus that all the world should be taxed.

2 (And this taxing was first made when Cyrenius was governor of Syria.)

3 And all went to be taxed, every one into his own city.

4 And Joseph also went up from Galilee, out of the city of Nazareth, into Judaea, unto the city of David, which is called Bethlehem; (because he was of the house and lineage of David:)

5 To be taxed with Mary his espoused wife, being great with child.

6 And so it was, that, while they were there, the days were accomplished that she should be delivered.

7 And she brought forth her firstborn son, and wrapped him in swaddling clothes, and laid him in a manger; because there was no room for them in the inn.

8 And there were in the same country shepherds abiding in the field, keeping watch over their flock by night.

9 And, lo, the angel of the Lord came upon them, and the glory of the Lord shone round about them: and they were sore afraid.

10 And the angel said unto them, Fear not: for, behold, I bring you good tidings of great joy, which shall be to all people.

11 For unto you is born this day in the city of David a Saviour, which is Christ the Lord.

12 And this shall be a sign unto you; Ye shall find the babe wrapped in swaddling clothes, lying in a manger.

13 And suddenly there was with the angel a multitude of the heavenly host praising God, and saying,

14 Glory to God in the highest, and on earth peace, good will toward men.

15 And it came to pass, as the angels were gone away from them into heaven, the shepherds said one to another, Let us now go even unto Bethlehem, and see this thing which is come to pass, which the Lord hath made known unto us.

16 And they came with haste, and found Mary, and Joseph, and the babe lying in a manger.

17 And when they had seen it, they made known abroad the saying which was told them concerning this child.

18 And all they that heard it wondered at those things which were told them by the shepherds.

19 But Mary kept all these things, and pondered them in her heart.

20 And the shepherds returned, glorifying and praising God for all the things that they had heard and seen, as it was told unto them.

21 And when eight days were accomplished for the circumcising of the child, his name was called JESUS, which was so named of the angel before he was conceived in the womb.

22 And when the days of her purification according to the law of Moses were accomplished, they brought him to Jerusalem, to present him to the Lord;

23 (As it is written in the law of the LORD, Every male that openeth the womb shall be called holy to the Lord;)

24 And to offer a sacrifice according to that which is said in the law of the Lord, A pair of turtledoves, or two young pigeons.

25 And, behold, there was a man in Jerusalem, whose name was Simeon; and the same man was just and devout, waiting for the consolation of Israel: and the Holy Ghost was upon him.

26 And it was revealed unto him by the Holy Ghost, that he should not see death, before he had seen the Lord's Christ.

27 And he came by the Spirit into the temple: and when the parents brought in the child Jesus, to do for him after the custom of the law,

28 Then took he him up in his arms, and blessed God, and said,

29 Lord, now lettest thou thy servant depart in peace, according to thy word:

30 For mine eyes have seen thy salvation,

31 Which thou hast prepared before the face of all people;

32 A light to lighten the Gentiles, and the glory of thy people Israel.

33 And Joseph and his mother marvelled at those things which were spoken of him.

34 And Simeon blessed them, and said unto Mary his mother, Behold, this child is set for the fall and rising again of many in Israel; and for a sign which shall be spoken against;

35 (Yea, a sword shall pierce through thy own soul also,) that the thoughts of many hearts may be revealed.

36 And there was one Anna, a prophetess, the daughter of Phanuel, of the tribe of Aser: she was of a great age, and had lived with an husband seven years from her virginity;

37 And she was a widow of about fourscore and four years, which departed not from the temple, but served God with fastings and prayers night and day.

38 And she coming in that instant gave thanks likewise unto the Lord, and spake of him to all them that looked for redemption in Jerusalem.

39 And when they had performed all things according to the law of the Lord, they returned into Galilee, to their own city Nazareth.

Matthew 2:1-23 (KJV)

1 Now when Jesus was born in Bethlehem of Judaea in the days of Herod the king, behold, there came wise men from the east to Jerusalem,

2 Saying, Where is he that is born King of the Jews? for we have seen his star in the east, and are come to worship him.

3 When Herod the king had heard these things, he was troubled, and all Jerusalem with him.

4 And when he had gathered all the chief priests and scribes of the people together, he demanded of them where Christ should be born.

5 And they said unto him, In Bethlehem of Judaea: for thus it is written by the prophet,

6 And thou Bethlehem, in the land of Juda, art not the least among the princes of Juda: for out of thee shall come a Governor, that shall rule my people Israel.

7 Then Herod, when he had privily called the wise men, enquired of them diligently what time the star appeared.

8 And he sent them to Bethlehem, and said, Go and search diligently for the young child; and when ye have found him, bring me word again, that I may come and worship him also.

9 When they had heard the king, they departed; and, lo, the star, which they saw in the east, went before them, till it came and stood over where the young child was.

10 When they saw the star, they rejoiced with exceeding great joy.

11 And when they were come into the house, they saw the young child with Mary his mother, and fell down, and worshipped him: and when they had opened their treasures, they presented unto him gifts; gold, and frankincense and myrrh.

12 And being warned of God in a dream that they should not return to Herod, they departed into their own country another way.

13 And when they were departed, behold, the angel of the Lord appeareth to Joseph in a dream, saying, Arise, and take the young child and his mother, and flee into Egypt, and be thou there until I bring thee word: for Herod will seek the young child to destroy him.

14 When he arose, he took the young child and his mother by night, and departed into Egypt:

15 And was there until the death of Herod: that it might be fulfilled which was spoken of the Lord by the prophet, saying, Out of Egypt have I called my son.

16 Then Herod, when he saw that he was mocked of the wise men, was exceeding wroth, and sent forth, and slew all the children that were in Bethlehem, and in all the coasts thereof, from two years old and under, according to the time which he had diligently inquired of the wise men.

17 Then was fulfilled that which was spoken by Jeremiah the prophet, saying,

18 In Rama was there a voice heard, lamentation, and weeping, and great mourning, Rachel weeping for her children, and would not be comforted, because they are not.

19 But when Herod was dead, behold, an angel of the Lord appeareth in a dream to Joseph in Egypt,

20 Saying, Arise, and take the young child and his mother, and go into the land of Israel: for they are dead which sought the young child's life.

21 And he arose, and took the young child and his mother, and came into the land of Israel.

22 But when he heard that Archelaus did reign in Judaea in the room of his father Herod, he was afraid to go thither: notwithstanding, being warned of God in a dream, he turned aside into the parts of Galilee:

23 And he came and dwelt in a city called Nazareth: that it might be fulfilled which was spoken by the prophets, He shall be called a Nazarene.

CHAPTER 2

Joseph's Testimony if Given Today (The Earthly Father of God's Son)

I am so very thankful that you invited me here today to share my testimony of what God has done in my life.

I am Joseph, and I was born in the lineage of David. From my childhood we went to the synagogue, and the rabbis taught us from the Torah the Jewish laws and what the great prophets that had gone before us had prophesied. We all knew that a Messiah was coming. It had been prophesied by many, and even the great prophet Isaiah prophesied: "The Lord himself shall give you a sign; Behold, a virgin shall conceive, and bear a son, and shall call His name Immanuel." We would rejoice and remind each other continually that our new King, the Messiah, our Deliverer, was coming. This was wonderful news! Our Messiah was coming, and we couldn't wait until that great day of our Messiah's appearance. All of us were in great anticipation of that day, and with the Romans in control, we all knew that it had to be soon.

I considered myself so very blessed; I was not only from the lineage of David, but I was engaged to the most beautiful young woman in our village. Our marriages were prearranged by our parents. When my father and mother told me who they had chosen to be my wife, and her parents agreed on the contract, I knew that I had favor with God, and that He had blessed me! Mary was a beautiful young woman with a lovely spirit and a sense of humor, too. She was wonderful, and I couldn't believe she was going to be my wife! I was so excited; my dear Mary. I could hardly wait until the day that I could take her as my bride. Plus, God had blessed my business. I was a carpenter, and I had built her a beautiful home. A great future I had started to plan for Mary and me.

Then one day, Mary came to me and said she had something vitally important to tell me. Mary said, "An angel appeared to me and said I should fear not, for I had found favor with God, and blessed was I above all women. The angel said that I was going to have a child, and it was going to be God's Son." So Mary said she had told the angel that she was a handmaid of the Lord, and let it be unto her according to His word. Then she said the words that caused me to see my whole world unraveling: "So, I am carrying a child."

Well, come on now, which one of you men would have believed such a story? I know that it has been prophesied, but would you believe that? If your girlfriend, your fiancee, came to you and told you that, would you believe her? I thought, *How could this happen? I love her so much; what did she do? Did she betray me?* I was broken-hearted. Plus, according to Jewish law, we could both be stoned. My dear Mary, who I fell in love with and thought I knew and trusted. The woman who I had been working hard to prepare a future for and planning to spend the rest of my life with. Now, she tells me she is going to have a baby! And I know that it's not mine. Oh! But I couldn't give her away; I couldn't have her stoned. In that day, when you were engaged, it was like being married, and you had to get a divorce. So I decided to give her away privately. I wasn't going to make a spectacle of her. I didn't want Mary stoned or hurt in any way; I loved Mary. I just couldn't be a part of this; I couldn't let people think I'd had any role in getting her pregnant. Oh my goodness, my mind was going a hundred miles a minute. How could this be?

Then Mary told me, "I am going to see my cousin Elisabeth, because the angel told me that she is with child and is in her sixth month." Well, we all knew that she was too old to have a baby. Zacharias and she had tried for years, but could not have a baby. When Mary returned, she told me that Elisabeth said that when she heard her voice, the baby in her womb leaped with joy, and Elisabeth was filled with the Holy Ghost. Elisabeth spake with a loud voice, saying, "Blessed art thou among women, and blessed is the fruit of thy womb. How am I so privileged that the mother of my Lord would come to me?"

I was in amazement at how Elisabeth had confirmed to Mary what the angel had told her. Then one night, an angel appeared to me and said, "Take Mary as your wife; the child that she carries is from the Lord, and He has chosen her to be the mother of His child." Oh, she was telling me the truth. Mary had told me she had asked the angel how this could be, when she knew not a man. The angel had said to Mary that nothing was impossible with God. *Nothing* is impossible with God! Now God has chosen me, too. All these prophesies that I have read and heard about all my life, and God has chosen me to be a part of His Master plan! Now, everything had changed. I began to realize that Mary was not only loved and chosen by me, but that God had also chosen her and loved her. I was so excited, and I went to Mary and told her that an angel had appeared to me and told me to take her as my wife, and that what she had told me was the truth.

Well, when we said yes to the Lord, our plans all fell by the wayside. God had a different plan for our lives. We had read in Jeremiah 29:11 that He knew the plans He had for us, declares the Lord. Plans to prosper us and to bring us to an expected end. But now, to be a part of His plan—and Mary had said yes, and now I said yes. So I took my dear Mary to be my wife.

By this time, Mary was really pregnant, and the Roman government passed a decree that required every man to return to their birthplace to take a census and pay taxes. Since I was born in Bethlehem, it would take at least four to five days to make this eighty-mile journey. How could Mary go with me? But Mary, my dear Mary, said, "I am going with you. We are not going to be apart." And I had to agree, since I could not stand even the thought of being apart from Mary, either. You know how it is when you love someone. So we went, and the trip went very well. When we arrived in Bethlehem, I knocked on the door of every inn, inquiring whether they had any available rooms. Now, I am not poor; my business is very successful, and I'm blessed. I had money to pay for the inn, but I was surprised at the crowd of people that had traveled to Bethlehem to take the census and pay their taxes. It was like what you would experience when you have a Notre Dame game in South Bend. You could not find a room at one of your hotels or motels if you tried. That is how it was there in Bethlehem; we could not find any rooms. Finally, a man felt sorry for us, seeing how pregnant my wife was, and said he had a stable where the animals were kept that he would let us use. He said it would be a warm shelter and get us out of the night air. He said he would put down some clean hay, and we could stay as long as we needed. So I thanked him, but I thought, *Why is my Mary going to a stable? She is pregnant with the Christ child.* Upon arrival, we found it to be a very nice stable. God provides, and when God takes care of you, He does it differently than what you could ever read or declare, because God is good.

We weren't there very long before Mary started to go into labor. She gave birth to a beautiful Son. It was amazing to be a part of all of this, and while we were getting used to holding our new Son, admiring the wonderful, wonderful blessing we had just been given. Can you imagine holding the Son of God and kissing His face? Oh my, the anointing—the presence of God that was there with us—was so real. Suddenly, there was a knock at the door. It was some shepherds, and they asked if we had a newborn baby with us. One of the shepherds said, "We were out in the fields tending our sheep, and the angels appeared to us in the sky saying, 'Glory to God in the highest, and on earth peace, good will towards men.' The angels told us about the child and said that we would find Him here. So we have come to worship our Newborn King, and to see Him for ourselves." We were astonished that God would send angels to proclaim His Son's birth in the whole sky. I can't even begin to explain the overwhelming gratitude and praise that I felt at that moment, just to know that other people had been looking forward to the Messiah's arrival for years and years, and that God had let us be part of all of it. Oh, how exciting! So we let the shepherds come in and worship their Newborn King.

On the eighth day, by Jewish custom, a male child must be circumcised. At that time, I told them that His name will be called Jesus. For the angel Gabriel had told Mary, before she had conceived, that she should call His name Jesus. So we didn't even have to think about it; God had named His Son.

When Jesus was forty days old, we traveled from Bethlehem to the temple in Jerusalem to present Jesus to the Lord. This was after the days of Mary's purification were accomplished, according to the Law of Moses. The law of the Lord says that every male that opens the womb shall be called holy to the Lord, and to offer a sacrifice, which is a pair of turtledoves or two young pigeons.

When we entered the temple in Jerusalem, we were greeted by Simeon, who was a devout man of God. Simeon told us that the Holy Ghost had told him that he would not see death before he had seen the Lord's Christ. He told us that the Spirit had told him to come to the temple right then. He took Jesus in his arms and blessed God, and said, "Lord, now let thou thy servant depart in peace, according to thy word: for mine eyes have seen thy salvation, which thou hast prepared before the face of all people; a light to lighten the Gentiles, and the glory of thy people Israel."

Mary and I marveled at what Simeon had just prophesied over Jesus, and what God had revealed to him. Then Simeon came over and blessed us. He then turned to Mary and said: "Behold, this child is set for the fall and rising again of many in Israel; and for a sign which shall be spoken against; yea, a sword shall pierce through thy own soul also, that the thoughts of many hearts may be revealed." We looked at each other with amazement, wondering what all of this meant.

Upon another visit to the temple in Jerusalem, a widow named Anna, who was a prophetess and served God in the temple by fastings and prayers night and day, approached us. She gave thanks unto the Lord and continued to talk about Jesus to all that looked for redemption in Jerusalem.

We were right there in the middle of one prophecy after another, opening up before our eyes. Prophesies we had heard and read about for years—and God let us be a part of it.

With Jesus being little, I decided we would stay in Bethlehem for a while. So, I started another business, and Mary found a home that she liked. Then one night, three wise men arrived at our house, along with all their crew that they had traveling with them. A star had settled over our home, and we were so amazed. The wise men said that they had been traveling for two years, following the star—two years, because they watched these kinds of signs. They had gone to Herod, and Herod had the chief priests and scribes search the prophecies to see where the king was to be born. They reported back to Herod that the prophets had written that He would be born in Bethlehem of Judea. Just as was prophesied, there we were. Isn't that amazing? We were doing what God asked us to do, and we were right in the middle of God's will. It had been prophesied years before—and there we were. The wise men brought us wonderful gifts of gold, and frankincense, and myrrh. These three wise men laid their gifts at the feet of Jesus, and they knelt down and worshiped Him as King. They weren't all Jews either; hmm.

We went to bed that night, astonished at what we had just experienced. I had not been sleeping very long before an angel appeared to me and said: "Joseph, you need to take the child and His mother and go to Egypt to protect Him." When the angel gave me these instructions, I didn't wait another minute. I didn't say, "We have a house, and I have established a business here." I got up and immediately, that night, took my family, and we went to Egypt. When God tells you to do something, it might not always be what you want or what you had planned. But His ways are the best, and they are always right. I was finding things that were way beyond what I could ever comprehend in my life happening to me. To think that I was a part of His almighty plan, and that God trusted me enough to be a part of it.

So, we traveled into Egypt, and we stayed there until an angel of the Lord came to me in a dream and told me to go back to the land of Israel, because Herod was dead. When we returned, I heard that Herod's son reigned, and I was afraid. But God warned me in a dream to turn and go into parts of Galilee, and so we returned to our hometown of Nazareth. I had thought many times of never going back to Nazareth, due to the many issues surrounding our marriage and baby. You know how people talk; some never seem to forget anything. But by this time, I had come to trust that when God tells you to do something, He takes care of it and makes everything good. Later, I found out that it was to fulfill another prophesy: that the Messiah would be called a Nazarene.

Now, standing here today, I can tell you that not many of you remember your great-great-great-grandfather's name. Not many of you remember the ancestors that have gone on before you. I don't know if I could tell you my great-great-great-grandfather's name. But I can tell you this: God said that you would always remember Mary's name, and you still remember her. And you even remember me—sometimes more than once a year, but at least once a year. And every year, the world celebrates Jesus' birth, because God declared it, and when God wants His Son's birth remembered, it is.

Going on in the scriptures, you have been promised something bigger. You are still looking for the Messiah. The Messiah has come; God's Son came and laid down His life freely for you, so He could redeem you from your sins. Jesus knew what He was doing when He came here to earth. He knew exactly what He was born to do. You see, once a year, we had to take a lamb or a token to the priest to have it slain for our sins. But through Jesus coming as a baby, being obedient to His Father

God and going to the cross to pay for our sins, if you just believe in Him and ask Him to forgive you, your sins are forgiven. He also said something else, which was ours even in the Old Testament: that the blessings of God will come and overtake you.

When you come to Him, you come to Him not only for forgiveness of sins, but for a turnaround in your life. When you start following Him, you are never the same. Never! He does an inside work, and then when He asks for you to do things, you do it because of your love for Him. Because He has proven Himself time, after time, after time for you. He makes it personal to you. Sometimes you feel like you're the only one—that you're just in His presence, and He loves you so much because you are His favorite. He makes every one of us feel like that. Just awesome, how God can do that!

You see, it hasn't stopped. You are still looking for the Messiah. He is in your heart, but you are looking for His return this time. He's coming again. He is coming again; He is coming soon. He is coming for His redeemed, and they are going to be caught up in the air, to live with Him forever. We thought that our Messiah was coming to be the King of this world, but God showed us that He was coming to be the King of our hearts, and to be King for all eternity. You can see that it has not stopped; you are still looking for the prophecies to be fulfilled. The prophecies will come to pass, and just as I was a part of them, you are a part of them. He is coming again. He is coming again; get ready! Get ready! Get ready! He is coming like that! Just like we didn't know when He was coming, but we kept on looking for Him and expecting His arrival at any time—enthusiastically waiting for His appearance.

Confidently know that you are a part of His almighty plan and our Messiah's return, when you will be caught up to be with Him forever. But in the meantime, go tell—just like I am telling—go tell what God has done for you through Jesus Christ. He asked for every one of you to make it your testimony. The Word says that we overcome by the blood of the Lamb, which is Jesus, and the word of our testimony. Stay real close, knowing that you are a part of His Master plan. He has chosen you, and He does have an excellent plan for your life, too. He will speak to you through His Word (the Bible), in your spirit, by angels, or by prophecy. He is still speaking today, and we are still looking for His return.

Until that day, we will stand and love Him! And adore Him! And praise Him! Because we have made Him the Lord of our lives, and Jesus was willing to come to earth and pay for us.

Hallelujah! Hallelujah! Hallelujah!

Praise His holy name!

Closing Words

Only when we get to heaven can we hear Joseph's true testimony. I stayed true to the biblical account of the birth of Jesus. My hope is that this story helps make the Bible come alive and be real to you.

May the Holy Spirit ignite in you a passion and a hunger for the Word of God. As Jesus said in Matthew 5:6 (KJV), "Blessed are they which do hunger and thirst after righteousness: for they shall be filled."

Just as written in Joseph's testimony, we are still looking for our Messiah's return, but this time he will return as King Jesus, to reign for all eternity. He will gather all those who have believed in their hearts and received Him into the kingdom of God.

If you have never accepted Jesus as your Messiah, I hope today that you make a decision to accept Him as your personal Lord and Savior. It will be the very best decision that you have ever made in your life. It is a decision that starts with believing in your heart and declaring with your mouth. Romans 10:9-11 (KJV) makes it very clear and says, "That if thou shalt confess with thy mouth the Lord Jesus, and shalt believe in thine heart that God hath raised him from the dead, thou shalt be saved. For with the heart man believeth unto righteousness; and with the mouth confession is made unto salvation. For the scripture saith, Whosoever believeth on him shall not be ashamed."

John 3:16 (KJV): "For God so loved the world, that he gave his only begotten Son, that whosoever believeth in him should not perish, but have everlasting life."

This is a salvation prayer written by my pastor, Dr. Lester Sumrall.

Please say it with your mouth and believe it in your heart:

O God in heaven, I come to you a sinner: I thank you for sending Jesus to die for me. I call upon Jesus now to come into my heart and save me. In Jesus' name. Amen.

Romans 10:13 (KJV) "For whosoever shall call upon the name of the Lord shall be saved."

If I don't get to meet you on earth, I know that I will meet you in heaven.

Appendix

To all the adoptive parents on this earth who have children that they truly love and thank God for every day.

As I was meditating on the Word of God one day, and on the generations of Jesus Christ, I was captivated by the thought of how God grafted Jesus into the genealogy of Joseph, and not Mary.

It reminded me of how, in Romans 8:14-17, it says that we are adopted into the family of God through Jesus Christ and are joint-heirs with Him. We have received the Spirit of adoption, whereby we cry Abba, Father (Daddy, God).

Romans 8:14-17 (KJV):

> *"For as many as are led by the Spirit of God, they are the sons of God. For ye have not received the spirit of bondage again to fear; but ye have received the Spirit of adoption, whereby we cry, Abba, Father. The Spirit itself beareth witness with*

our spirit, that we are the children of God: And if children, then heirs; heirs of God, and joint-heirs with Christ; if so be that we suffer with him, that we may be also glorified together."

The child is now under his adoptive father's genealogy, just like we, as born-again believers, are grafted into the generations of God.

Ephesians says that God chose us before the world was formed, and predestined us to be adopted through Jesus Christ to be His children. This was done to give our heavenly Father pleasure. This is just like our children that are either biologically, or by adoption, ours.

Ephesians 1:4-5 (KJV):

"According as he hath chosen us in him before the foundation of the world, that we should be holy and without blame before him in love: Having predestinated us unto the adoption of children by Jesus Christ to himself, according to the good pleasure of his will."

It is a wonderful feeling to be chosen and born again I hope this spoke to your heart like it did to mine.

Priestly Blessing

Numbers 6:24-26 (KJV):

> "The Lord bless thee, and keep thee: The Lord make
> his face shine upon thee, and be gracious unto thee:
> The Lord lift up his countenance upon thee, and
> give thee peace."

Jude 1:24-25 (KJV):

> "Now unto him that is able to keep you from falling,
> and to present you faultless before the presence of
> his glory with exceeding joy, To the only wise God
> our Saviour, be glory and majesty, dominion and
> power, both now and ever. Amen."

Notes

Proverbs 22:6 (KJV)

> *"Train up a child in the way he should go: and when he is old, he will not depart from it."*

Isaiah 7:14 (KJV)

> *"Therefore the Lord himself shall give you a sign; Behold, a virgin shall conceive, and bear a son, and shall call his name Immanuel."*

Jeremiah 29:11 (KJV)

> *"For I know the thoughts that I think toward you, saith the Lord, thoughts of peace, and not of evil, to give you an expected end."*

Luke 1:48 (KJV)

> *"For he hath regarded the low estate of his handmaiden: for, behold, from henceforth all generations shall call me blessed."*

John 3:16 (KJV)

> *"For God so loved the world, that he gave his only begotten Son, that whosoever believeth in him should not perish, but have everlasting life."*

Revelation 4:1-2 (KJV)

> *"After this I looked, and, behold, a door was opened in heaven: and the first voice which I heard was as it were of a trumpet talking with me; which said, Come up hither, and I will shew thee things which must be hereafter. And immediately I was in the spirit: and, behold, a throne was set in heaven, and one sat on the throne."*

Revelation 7:9-17 (KJV)

> *"After this I beheld, and, lo, a great multitude, which no man could number, of all nations, and kindreds, and people, and tongues, stood before the throne, and before the Lamb, clothed with white robes, and palms in their hands; And cried with a loud voice, saying, Salvation to our God which sitteth upon the throne, and unto the Lamb. And all the angels stood round about the throne, and about the elders and the four beasts, and fell before the throne on their faces, and worshipped God, Saying, Amen: Blessing, and glory, and wisdom,*

and thanksgiving, and honour, and power, and might, be unto our God for ever and ever. Amen. And one of the elders answered, saying unto me, What are these which are arrayed in white robes? and whence came they? And I said unto him, Sir, thou knowest. And he said to me, These are they which came out of great tribulation, and have washed their robes, and made them white in the blood of the Lamb. Therefore are they before the throne of God, and serve him day and night in his temple: and he that sitteth on the throne shall dwell among them. They shall hunger no more, neither thirst any more; neither shall the sun light on them, nor any heat. For the Lamb which is in the midst of the throne shall feed them, and shall lead them unto living fountains of waters: and God shall wipe away all tears from their eyes."

Revelation 11:15-17 (KJV)

"And the seventh angel sounded; and there were great voices in heaven, saying, The kingdoms of this world are become the kingdoms of our Lord, and of his Christ; and he shall reign for ever and ever. And the four and twenty elders, which sat before God on their seats, fell upon their faces, and worshipped God, Saying, We give thee thanks, O

*Lord God Almighty, which art, and wast, and art
to come; because thou hast taken to thee thy great
power, and hast reigned."*

Revelation 12:11 (KJV)

*"And they overcame him by the blood of the Lamb,
and by the word of their testimony; and they loved
not their lives unto the death."*

Everybody has a story... go tell your story.

CPSIA information can be obtained
at www.ICGtesting.com
Printed in the USA
JSHW040824260520
5887JS00006B/45